THIS SCEPTER'D ISLE

Shakespeare in praise of Britain

with photographs by
FAY GODWIN

SOUVENIR PRESS

This royal throne of kings,

this scepter'd isle,

This earth of majesty,

this seat of Mars,

This other Eden, demi-paradise;

This fortress, built by Nature for herself,
Against infection, and the hand of war;

This happy breed of men,

this little world;

This precious stone set in the silver sea,

Which serves it in the office of a wall,
Or as a moat defensive to a house,

Against the envy of less happier lands;

This blessed plot, this earth, this realm, this England . . .

This land of such dear souls, this dear, dear land . . .

England, bound in with the triumphant sea,

Whose rocky shore beats back the envious siege
Of watery Neptune.